# Happy?

### How To Win The
### *Lasting* Happiness
### That You Desire

Happy?
Sherman Joseph
Copyright © 2014 by Sherman and Bilon Joseph
Published by JAMA Publishing
Gainesville, Florida 32669

Visit our Web site at www.jamapublishing.com

JAMA is an imprint of JAMA Publishing.
The JAMA name and logo are trademarks of JAMA Publishing, Inc.

Printed in the United States of America

First Edition: April 2014
10  9  8  7  6  5  4  3  2  1

 ISBN 978-0-9960793-1-0

# DEDICATION

To Bilon - For Believing in me and for
Challenging me to be the man God has
called me to be.

To Maya and Jackie - For your inspiration.

To Nanny - For your unconditional love and
support.

To Mom - For giving me life.

# —— CONTENTS ——

# INTRODUCTION

I am sure at some point in your life you have heard the saying, 'don't worry be happy'. When you think about it, it is really some good advice, especially when you find yourself going through a difficult time. Yet, to our own stubbornness, many of us can find it difficult to follow such a simple task. It shouldn't be so hard, but somehow it is.

With everything that is going on around us, from the killings of young people in the United States to the wars in the Middle East, it is no surprise that so many people find it hard to just be happy. Instead, too often we may find ourselves reaching out in harmful ways to find the happiness that we desire without any true success.

I know all of this may seem discouraging so far, but don't fret; I have some outstanding news for you. Awesome news, in fact! If you desire to find joy, peace, and happiness, you are in the right place at the right time.

I recall my time working at a homeless shelter in Orlando, Florida. Every morning on my way into the office, I would encounter an elderly homeless gentleman who happened to be a resident at this very shelter. He would always have a smile on his face, and greet me with, "Good morning, Mr. Joseph. Today is going to be a great day!" For the life of me, I could not understand why this guy was so happy. I mean he spent his nights sleeping on a hard gym floor, if he was lucky enough to find a spot, or outside in downtown Orlando.

One day he stopped and asked me this question: "Mr. Joseph, I spent last night watching people coming and going to an Orlando Magic game. They seemed to have everything in the world, yet many of them seemed to also be so unhappy. How is it that they can have everything in the world, but yet still don't have happiness?" I could not answer him. I soon began to look around at some of my clients who for the most part were very pleasant people. So I wondered to myself, how some people could be happy despite being in what may seem like bad conditions to most, while others, who seemed to have everything going well for them, were so unhappy.

So I started to study this more, especially during my time working at the shelter. Looking at the two sets of people and the way they approached life, the answer to the question about happiness became quite clear to me: it's all about perspective! You see, God has given every man something called free-will. With this free-will we are able to choose how we want to approach life. We can equally control certain aspects of our lives, deciding to make choices about the life that we want to live. If we make the right choices, chances are we will still be able to smile at the end of the day no matter what obstacles we face. But, on the other hand, we also have the choice to do the opposite, which at the end of the day can lead to great heartache and pain.

No matter what you have chosen, this guide will help you become more empowered to make new choices that will improve the quality of your life today!

I am so excited that you are here! I look forward to sharing with you some nuggets that I have learned and used to help get on track to enjoying the life that I live today despite the obstacles that I may face.

I promise you that if you take the time to not just read what I have written but to also put in the work, you will begin to have a different outlook on life, and things will change for the better. I am not talking about some small change, but a drastic change, a revolutionary change! The only request that I have of you is that you approach these ideas with an open-mind and a positive attitude. Remember, it is all up to you. You have to be willing to take the necessary steps with what you learn. I can be your guide, but I cannot do the work for you.

Happiness is so contagious. It is like yawning. Have you ever been around someone and they yawned? Next thing you know, you are yawning too! The same thing goes with being around happy people.

Don't be surprised when your family, friends, and co-workers start to wonder what in the world has gotten into you. You start to enjoy going to work. You begin to get raises and promotions. Doors start to open for you. It is amazing how your attitude can affect the whole outcome of your life!

Take this book, re-read it if you need to. Take your time with it. This is your new tool that can be used for your seemingly never ending search for happiness. As long as your effort is there, there is nothing that can get in your way.

I am so thankful to take this journey with you. I know you will go above and beyond your wildest expectations!

So let's not hold off any longer. We do not want to waste another moment!

# ── 1 ──

# ARE YOU HAPPY?

*He that handles a matter wisely shall find good: and whoever trusts in the LORD, happy is he.*
                                    —Proverbs 16:20

So are you happy? I guess that depends on who you ask and what you define happiness as. If you are unhappy, it is an important factor to understand why before you can attempt to solve the problem.

Now it is completely possible that you have such a unique issue that's causing this unhappiness. But more often than not, it is not someone or something else causing this unhappiness, it is that you may be bringing this unhappiness upon yourself. If this is the case, some time spent alone doing some self-reflection could do some good.

I believe that introspection will help you get to the root of the problem. I have provided a list to help you in this process. This list is comprised of things that have been known to bring many of us down, including myself. As I have said before, if you can get an understanding about what is causing the problem, you can develop the game plan needed to overcome it!

## Worry Warts

Have you ever been around someone, and no matter what is going on in their life they are always worrying about something. They can never seem to find peace. Life could be going well, but yet they still will find something to worry about. Could this person be you?

Do you go to dinner with your spouse but spend the evening worry about what the kids are doing at home? Or do you worry how you are going to pay the bills? Do you spend days, weeks, nights, worrying about things that you really don't have any control over? However, what would your life be like if you spent it enjoying your loved ones and the things around you? People who worry a lot tend to worry about things that they cannot change. So stop wasting your time. Worrying is not going to solve your problem. I know you are smarter than this. There are more constructive ways that you can spend your time. The earth is a beautiful place, so enjoy it!

## Social Media Highlight Reels

With the easy access of social media, we are able to see into the lives of our friends, celebrities, and whomever else we are interested in finding out about. The problem with this is that we can begin to compare ourselves to what someone else is doing.

Happiness is not at all about what you don't have and what someone else does, even though society is trying to sell you on the idea that material objects will bring you happiness. For instance, if your friend goes out and purchases a new Lexus and posts it on social media and you decide to go out and do the same thing, is this going to bring you happiness? You may enjoy it for a little while, but I bet that you won't find the same joy in it that your friend has, especially if you can't afford it. Not only are you left to deal with comparing yourself to your friend, but now you have added an unnecessary expense to the mix of your problems.

You have to understand that God placed you on this earth to become the best *you* that you can be. Not to be the best someone else or what the media tells you that you need to be. Do not spend your time caught up in the highlight reel of others. You do not know the sacrifice and the price they had to pay to get to where they are. Focus on creating your own highlight reel and being your best self.

## Who's In Your Circle?

I remember growing up as child and always hearing my grandparents tell me 'you have to watch the people that you hang around.' My grandmother is a very strict person. Even to this day, she keeps a watchful eye on everything, especially my two daughters. Even though I thought she was being over- protective of me when I was a child, as an adult, I understand what she was doing. You have to watch who you decide to hang around. Negativity is a virus that can spread like wild fire. There is no contraceptive that you can use against it. It is something that you have to be extremely aware of at all times. So protect yourself by any means necessary.

The best way to do this is to look at your circle. If you are surrounded by people who don't ever have anything positive to say, who always complains about what they don't have, or who talks about what they are going to do but never takes action to actually do anything, then I suggest it is time to make some new friends.

Additionally, if you are always the smartest person in your circle, then it is time to change your circle. You will always have people pulling on you for something, but if you don't have anyone who can pour into your life, this can become very draining. We all need people who can give more than they take.

## What Are You Eating?

I can attest to this. I was at the heaviest that I ever been in my life: 325lbs. Boy was I in shock. How did this happen. With my height, it was easy to fool myself, because it does not always show so easily. However, when I saw that number and returned from the doctor's office, I felt like my life was over. I wanted to give up. But I had to remind myself that I did this to myself and that no one else was to blame for this.

I was a product of what I ate. If you notice those who take pride in their health are very conscientious about the food that they put into their bodies. When you have a poor diet and no exercise, you are allowing for unhappiness to grow within you. You only have one body; you have to take great care of it. It is your temple, so treat it as such. We'll visit this principle more in *Chapter 7 Health Matters.*

I know this list isn't exhaustive, but I am sure you can find some areas within it that you could work on. Identifying the problem is the first step to overcoming. It is not impossible; happiness is right there waiting on you.

# 2

# A VALUABLE YOU

*I praise you because I am fearfully and wonderfully made; your works are wonderful, I know that full well.*

—Psalm 139:14

T oo often we find ourselves in meaningless relationships. We spend so much time trying to hold on to them because we may feel this is the best we can do, or maybe that we can change the other person in the relationship. However we are really hurting inside. In order to truly love someone else, you have to first love yourself. In order to love yourself and to understand your value, you must learn to look at yourself the same way Jesus would look at you. He sees past your faults and failures.

Learning to love the person that you see in the mirror will make it easier with any other struggles that you may face. Overcoming self-esteem issues can often seem almost impossible to overcome; trust me I have been there. However, with time and with the tools that you learn, it is possible to do!

Allow me to share some pointers that I used to overcome my own struggle with self-esteem and self-worth. I encourage you to take these points that you are given and put them into action. You will be pleasantly surprised by the results.

## Be Proud Of Your Wins

Critiquing every little thing that you do or don't do is a common task of many people. Truly, if you are always striving for greatness, it is not uncommon to fall into this trap. You may look at friends, family, or role models and see what they are accomplishing and feel like you may not add up to where they are. However, you have to learn to be your biggest fan wherever you are no matter how big or small the accomplishment maybe.

Remember, you are taking steps, and as long as you are moving, then you truly have something to be proud of. Stop blowing off your accomplishments, and simply give you the credit that you deserve.

## Who Says You Are Ugly

It is funny how so many people spend so much time looking at people on TV or the internet and allow them to determine the way they should look, dress, or act. Yet, if you ask some "beautiful" person how does he/she feels about themselves it is not uncommon to hear them say that they are not happy with the way they look. Take Halle Berry...most people would say she is a drop-dead gorgeous woman. However, according to an article published by *Essence Magazine*, she was extremely insecure about her looks. But on the contrary, you have someone like Biggie Smalls who most people would say was not that attractive, yet he had this confidence about him to win the affection of some very beautiful women. So if you find yourself looking in the mirror and thinking you are not attractive, then I want you to stop and remind yourself that there are indeed some people who would strongly disagree with you.

## Let Go Of The Past

How many times have you given your heart to the wrong person or maybe you jumped into a business venture with someone that you should not have. How much time are you spending living in the past in regards to this decision? This is not an uncommon practice, yet it can be a costly one.

We all make mistakes. It is a part of life. You have to learn to embrace the mistakes that you have made. There can always be a positive outcome of any situation, no matter how bad you may think it is. If you loved the wrong person, now you know what qualities that you don't want in a mate. Just be patient with the process. Give yourself time to grow and learn. If you learn to let go of your past and become more patient with yourself, you will see how much stress and pressure just falls off of your life.

## Treat Yourself

All work and no play leads to a very dull and boring life. Take some time to treat yourself. When you learn to treat yourself better, you are saying that you are going to love yourself more. Not only are you saying this to yourself, but you are also sharing this with the world. When people see that you treat yourself well and you love yourself, you are telling them that they need to treat you with the same respect. One thing I always tell my daughters, if a man can't do for you what daddy can do, then he is not worth your time. Now I know they are only five and three, however, I want them to learn at an early age how to value themselves.

Are you doing anything nice for yourself? Maybe it could be taking you out to dinner or to a movie. Maybe you want to go purchase a new outfit or some fishing gear. Whatever the case maybe, you must take time out to treat yourself.

If this is something that you are not doing, I highly encourage you to start. Why are you working so hard in the first place if you can't enjoy it? So start with one day out of the month and do something for yourself. If you truly love yourself, then you deserve to treat yourself this way. If you are not happy and complete, you will be no good to anyone else.

These suggestions are very simple to do, but they are going to take work. Nevertheless, changing the way you see yourself is does not have to be a complicated task. You don't need medication to do it. Loving you and happiness go hand in hand. Give these suggestions a try and watch how you'll grow each day towards a better you!

# 3

# GRATITUDE

*Do not be anxious about anything, but in everything, by prayer and petition, with thanksgiving, present your requests to God.*

—Phillipians 4:6

There is so much power in being grateful. It is another important part to being happy and also an area where most people who are unhappy are most likely neglecting.

If you have ever found yourself struggling in this area, then begin to use these practical steps to help you start heading in the right direction.

**A Gratitude Journal**

Keep a notebook near your bed. When you wake in the morning and after your prayer time, write down a few things that you are grateful for. Be as creative as you would like. It is your own personal journal.

Just before bed, pull out your journal and reflect upon the things that you wrote that morning. Take some time now to also write down some things that you are grateful for that has happened throughout the day. Strive to do this exercise for at least 30 days without interruption.

See how you feel at the end of the 30 days. Many people choose to continue well beyond that time.

## Help Those in Need

"Generous hands are blessed hands because they give bread to the poor." (Proverbs 22:9, Message). As we can see from scripture, God has intended for man to help those who are less fortunate. In addition to this, generosity can also create a happier life for you.

Life happens to all of us, and I am sure you have had your fair share of tough times, but you can be assured that there is someone out there doing worse than you. The best way to get started with helping someone else could be to spend sometime at a homeless shelter, sit with someone who is in Hospice, or if you are an animal lover, you could spend some time at your local animal shelter.

Not only will these acts of kindness put a smile on someone else's face, but they will also help you to feel happier within yourself.

## Time With Family and Friends

As we grow and go about our lives, it is not uncommon for us to fall into the trap of taking our loved ones for granted. Chances are we don't necessarily do it on purpose; however, we tend to get so focused on what is going on around us. In reality, these are the ones that we should appreciate the most.

When times get hard or when you need someone to celebrate with, these are the individuals that you can turn to. So take some time to let those who are close to you know how important they are to you and how grateful you are to have them in your life. They deserve it don't you think?

## 'Thank You' Can Go A Long Way

It is amazing what a simple thank you can get you. Just by saying it to someone can set off a chain reaction that can lead to a happier experience for you.

It seems like in today's society fewer and fewer people have manners or are courteous to one another. When you show this type of respect to others, you create such a circle of positive energy that can be rejuvenating. All you did was just smile and say thank you. And, yes, it is that simple! So be kind and share a smile with someone today, and see how it will make you feel.

This may seem like such a small adjustment to the way we act, speak, or think. Yet they all add up over time. The more you put it into practice, the more you will notice yourself being happier and those around you will notice it as well.

Creating a great attitude is an important part of the equation. As you take the time to work towards it, you will find the results to be outstanding!

---- 4 ----

# THINK POSITIVE

*Finally, brothers, whatever is true, whatever is noble, whatever is right, whatever is pure, whatever is lovely, whatever is admirable--if anything is excellent or praiseworthy--think about such things.*

—Phillipians 4:6

The mind is such a powerful tool. It allows us to structure all of our life's experiences. How we choose to structure those experiences sets the stage for our emotional state which normally influences our next set of experiences.

If you can control the way you think, you can control the outcome of a lot of situations that you may find yourself in, whether they may be good or bad. Having a negative mindset creates a self-fulfilling prophecy. Often, we are not aware how we are contributing to our life of unhappiness with this mindset.

Think of your mind as the coach of a team. Whatever play you call, the team is going to execute. Is it going to be a play of happiness or are you going to give in because you find yourself down by a few points. When you choose to be positive and believe, the impossible task becomes possible! Follow these simple steps to help get you back on track:

## Music and Movies

It is so amazing how much music and movies play on our emotional state and how we view what is going on around us. Think about some of your favorite music growing up: how did it make you feel? I recall growing up, my mother loved to play James Brown. She would dance and sing to his songs all day while cleaning the house. Even though she was doing work that most people hated, this music put her in the mind-set to enjoy the task that she was doing.

But understand, you cannot listen or watch everything. You have to guard your spirit. What is playing in your mp3 player? What are you watching on T.V? Is it uplifting you or educating you? Does it allow you to think of all the possibilities that you could achieve, or does it do the opposite? You really have to pay close attention to things like this because you are more influenced by what you watch and listen to than you may be aware of.

If you conduct a self-assessment and note that what you feed your spirit with is negative or aggressive or simply a waste of your energy, consider doing a spring cleaning of a sort. Decide what you choose to expose yourself to. As humans, sometimes we take things like this for granted without realizing the effect that this has on our subconscious mind.

There is nothing wrong with entertainment. Just make sure you are not sacrificing your own potential by it.

### Knockout Negative Thoughts

Negative thoughts are going to happen. I wish they did not; but, the more you grow, the bigger they become. There will come a time when you doubt a choice that you make, but you have to get a handle on it quickly. You cannot let these thoughts take root.

By taking control of negative thoughts immediately and replacing them with something that is positive, you can prevent it having any real influence over you.

In order for this to work effectively you must channel your thoughts quickly. The longer you procrastinate and soak up those negative thoughts, the more harm they will do.

## Power in Affirmations

By now you should understand the power words play in your happiness. Let's take a deeper look into this to help channel our mindset.

"Death and life are in the power of the tongue, and those who love it will eat its fruits." (Proverbs 18:21 NIV) As we can see from the writings of King Solomon, the choice of words that we use in our lives can either bring us life or bring us death. That is why it is important to speak affirmations over your life daily.

An affirmation is a positive statement that you create and repeat to yourself when you wake in the morning, throughout the day when you feel stressed, and before going to bed at night.

When creating your own affirmation, please make sure that you write down things that you would like and appreciate, not negative things that you would like to avoid. For example, you would not say "I'm not ugly" you would say "I am beautiful and wonderfully made". This way, you allow the affirmations to take hold quicker and have a stronger effect. Your mind can play tricks on you.

Positive thinking creates a happier you. So try these suggestions and ideas, and enjoy the transformation that you will experience on your way to a happier you!

# 5

# DREAMS AND VISION

And afterward, I will pour out my Spirit on all people. Your sons and daughters will prophesy, your old men will dream dreams, your young men will see visions.

—Joel 2:28

I t is Monday morning, the alarm clock just began to chime. You struggle to get out of the bed because you hate going to this job that you are not passionate about.

This feeling is not uncommon in our society. It is believed that people are 20% more likely to suffer a heart attack on Monday than any other day of the week.

How often do you feel like you are just going through the motions? Whether it is working that dead end job or pursing a degree that you are not passionate about, this is one of the quickest ways to being consistently unhappy about life.

It does not matter how much money you will make or the prestige that may come with a degree, if you are not passionate about it, what is the point? Going this route, you are merely existing and not living. You have just put your life on auto pilot without any sense of purpose.

It is so easy to fall into this pit fall. I get it: rent has to be paid and you have to have food on the table. Those are things that you need to survive. So I do understand. That is why this area is one of the hardest to overcome. It is going to take some hard work, faith, and dedication to break free.

Nevertheless, don't be surprised if your family and friends don't support you through this transition. They may think you are crazy. However, it is your dream and not there's. God gave it to you and not them, so it is okay for them not to understand.

So I want you to think outside of the box. Do not allow money, education, or social class to keep you from dreaming big. Think about your purpose. Even if you don't think you have a purpose, you do. I believe God designed us all to fulfill a purpose here on earth. So think about your purpose and dreams. If you can do this, then half the battle is accomplished.

It is funny how as a child, you had so many big dreams. You never allowed limitations to get in your way. You would climb up or jump off of anything. However, it seems like the older you get the harder it is for you to have the same drive.

It is not too late. This problem does not have to consume your life any longer. Think about the following. It will help you along the way.

## Reflect Over the Past

The beauty about life is that you can always look back at the things that you have had to face. Everyone has had to face their own fork in the road. Some decisions worked out great and some did not. Yet you are still here today. If you find yourself struggling to find your purpose, take a look at your past. The answer to your purpose could be staring you in the face.

## Dream Big

Why dream small when you can dream big? No matter the dream, you should always dream big. Les Brown said it best when he stated: "People don't often fail because they dream too big. They often fail because they dream too small and hit"[2]. So don't be afraid to have big dreams.

It may take you sometime, step by step, to get to where you want to go. As long as you are moving toward your goal, you are heading in the right direction. The best way to go about this is to look for people who are living out there dreams. Follow what they do; learn from their own mistakes. You don't always have to reinvent the wheel. Find what is working for them and see how you can apply it to your own life.

## Enormous Faith

This journey can be a lonely one. You may even start to doubt yourself during this process, and you may even think you should check yourself in for a psychic evaluation.

Don't worry; you are not crazy. This road to happiness and purpose is traveled by few, unfortunately. So you won't find much traffic on it. This is where you have to rely on your faith during those long and lonely nights.

What God has given you is for you, so don't be afraid. It is time to find your purpose and to start living your dream.

# 6

# BE SOCIAL

*A man that has friends must show himself friendly.*

—Proverbs 18:24a

D o large crowds bother you? Are you uneasy about speaking to people that you don't know? Do you lie to yourself by saying you don't need people in your life to be happy? If you have, it is okay. It is not the end of the world; it is something that can be corrected. Studies have shown that 54% of the US population suffers from some form of anxiety in regards to public speaking[3]. These phobias can really do some damage to the quality of life you want to live if you do not get a handle on them.

For some people, being social does not come easy. It takes time and takes work to feel comfortable when interacting with strangers.

I was not always a social person. As a kid growing up, my grandfather and uncle would always get on me because I would not speak to people, or if I did speak, I would mumble as to where no one could hear what I was saying. I finally overcame this phobia in high school. You see, I had to take the time to work on my social skills.

Allow me to share with you some tips that have worked for me and for clients that I have worked with in the past. These tips can help you experience the same kind of personal revolution.

## Become Approachable

Smile! Nothing's wrong with it. It is funny when I hear people complaining that someone smiles too much. You never hear someone saying you have a beautiful frown.

If you are uncomfortable with speaking first to someone, then you should smile. This lets people know that you are friendly and social.

Also make sure you are aware of your body language. It is okay to unfold your arms; no one is trying to attack you. By unfolding your arms and standing erect sends such a positive vibe to others. It lets people know how friendly and confident you are.

## The Eyes Tell It All

I remember as child, my uncle would yell at me to look people in the eyes. I always thought he was crazy for this. It was not until I became older that I realized the importance of looking someone in the eyes. The eyes are said to be the window to a person's soul.

And for this reason, when you make eye contact while speaking to someone, you are letting them know you are confident in what you're saying. You will seem to be much more charismatic with your eye contact alone, as well.

Once I made it a habit to focus on this, it completely changed my life. I am sure it will do the same for you.

## Get Off Of The Couch

How often do you hear someone say "I am a loner" or "I don't need friends"? What they are really saying is I am lonely, and I don't know how to make friends.

We were not created to live life alone and in self-made box. Networking, relationships, and friends can be compared to football. It is a contact sport. You have to get out of your box in order to play, and I know you want to play!

The only way to deal with this is to become more social. If you struggle in this area, I suggest you make it habit to go out at least one night a week. If you are member of church, I would encourage that you get involved. You will meet all types of people.

After a few months of doing this, take a look and see all of the different people you have met and the relationships that you have built. I am sure you will be amazed!

Having a social life is having a happy life. You have to be willing to open the door and let people in. Once you do it, you will be glad that you did.

**Simple is Not Bad**

This is one area that I know far too well. I used to struggle with enjoying life to the fullest because I felt like I did not have the money to do the things that I wanted to do. If I could not do those things, then I was not going to do anything at all. I was trapped.

Society tends to tell us that we need to have the latest gadget, clothing, or toy to experience true happiness. Or that more likes on Twitter and Instagram would make us happier and successful.

I have learned that this is not true. Once I embraced enjoying life and those around me, the happier I became and the happier the people I loved were happy to be around me.

By enjoying what you have in life, your life has no choice but to become happier and more prosperous.

# 7

# HEALTH MATTERS

*For I will restore health unto you, and I will heal you of your wounds, says the LORD*

—Jeremiah 30:17a

Have you ever noticed that some of the happiest people in life are some of the fittest people. Being comfortable in your body is going to lead to you being happier about yourself and the way people look at you.

There have been studies that have shown that the more you eat right and exercise the happier you will be. One study conducted by Standford University showed that the act of moving around (running or walking) and some resistance training reduced incidents of depression[4].

Your level of physical fitness does not matter. Just being physically active will help with how you feel about yourself. We see it all the time on shows like the Biggest Loser.

So if you find yourself in this area and you want to start feeling more comfortable with the way you look and be happier within, follow these few points:

## Give Yourself Time

Rome was not built in a day and neither will the transformation of you occur instantly. It is going to take time. Some days it is going to hurt, but you can't give in and quit. Give yourself time, and work your way up because you are more likely to sustain this lifestyle change.

Moreover, it's okay to start small. Walk ten minutes a day. Do not park near the front of stores or your job. Take the stairs whenever you can.

Allow yourself time to build up strength and stamina.

## Ask For Help

If you live in a house with someone, let them know what you are trying to do, and ask them to help you reach your goals. Their support and potential participation will make your goal of being a healthier you that much more obtainable.

## Sudden Benefits

You will be surprised by the sudden benefits that you receive from regular exercise. You will start to have more energy. It may take time to see the results you desire in the mirror, certainly, but feeling happier and accomplished will likely hit you right away.

## More Opportunities To Be Happy

A healthy diet will give you more sustainable energy. More energy will give you the fuel you need to be active. And the more energy you have to devote to different areas of your life, the better they will run, and the happier you will be! Focusing on nutrition and exercise will truly reward you time and time again.

Remember, your body is your temple. Treat it as a friend and not a foe.

# ───── 8 ─────

## LOVED ONES

*And there is a friend that sticks closer than a brother.*

— Proverbs 18:24b

There is nothing better than having people around to share your wins and woes with. Going through life alone is damaging to the soul.

A blissful life is all about being around people we love and that care about us. This allows us the time to let down our guards and just laugh and enjoy each other's company. This is what life is all about.

## Having People To Count On

Have you ever been in a situation and you did not know how you were going to get out of it. Maybe there was a car accident, you just got arrested, or earned a bad grade in school. What did you do to get out of the situation? Most likely you asked someone for help. There is nothing like having people in your life that you can count on in times of need.

In order to find out who those people are, sometimes in life we have to remove some bad seeds. A part of the process of achieving happiness is to detoxify you of unnecessary stress and anxiety. Surrounding yourself with loved ones allows for some insulation from this type of pressure that drains you of your happiness and propels you forward towards reaching the goals that you are working to achieve.

Your friends and family will do all they can to help you when you are in need; however, sometimes we allow pride and ego to get in the way of that. Just knowing that you have people in your corner can be such a boost to both happiness and confidence in life, so don't be afraid to open yourself up to love and to be loved in return.

## Accept Constructive Critique

In most cases, you will always find at least one person who you know who cares enough about you to be brutally honest with you. This could be your brother, sister, uncle, cousin, pastor or friend. No matter who they are, they could be one of your most valuable resources. You see, they do not get pleasure in seeing you fail, but instead, they want the best for you.

Most people tend to struggle with this type of relationship. They feel that as a friend or family member, you should always agree with whatever they say or do. This is not their job.

Having access to this honest, though possibly painful, viewpoint may not seem like a source of happiness at the time, but in the long run, it is.

Living with this type of counsel can be challenging, but it is vital to your livelihood.

# 9

# The Ups and The Downs

*I consider that our present sufferings are not worth comparing with the glory that will be revealed in us.*

— Romans 8:18

I find it funny how people like to blame God because they are struggling or when things are not going their way. Yet, when things *are* going well, they are quick to say look what I did. The truth of the matter is that life is like being a farmer. You have to plant the seeds, teal the soil, water the ground, pull the weeds, and fertilize the land. You have to work your land. God never said life would be easy and perfect. No matter how we may try to escape life's ups and downs, in the end, we still have to face them.

What we can do is learn how to battle low points and how to cope with choppy waters without allowing ourselves to become depressed or dependent on destructive relationships or habits. Because when our heads is in the right place, we are prepared to deal with whatever life throws our way.

Here are few strategies I like to use to accept the challenges of life's ups and downs while still walking around with a smile on my face.

### Knowing All Things Will Pass

Jeremiah 29: 11 reminds us of God's plan for our lives: "For I know the plans I have for you, declares the Lord, plans to prosper you and not to harm you, plans to give you hope and a future". (NIV) Whenever you feel like things are going to be overwhelming, think about the promises that God has made over your life. Whatever you are going through at that time shall pass.

Think back to when you faced adversity in the past and you successfully overcame it. Everyone faces the situation that seems hopeless and appears like it will never end, but it does.

It's all about having the inner fortitude to continue to move forward and with a smile. Not only can this approach be beneficial to you, but it can also make you an inspiration to someone else. Everyone has a story, and we all can be examples for others when their chips are down.

## Keep Your Head Up

Pessimistic talking, defeated body language, and negative talk can be the worst enemy to your happiness. You can snatch victory out of the jaws of defeat by just making the choice to control these factors. Allow them to work for you and not against you.

Keep your head up. Again, walk upright and keep a smile on your face to allow your subconscious mind to be happy. Your mind is your strongest muscle. When you start feeling more positive, you will start to have more mental and physical resources available to you when times get tough.

## Enjoy The Good Times

It is so easy to get caught up in the negative things that life throws our way. We end up forgetting to enjoy the good times.

When things are going well for you, take the time to enjoy them. Truly enjoy it! Do not tell yourself that something negative is right around the corner. When you allow yourself to enjoy the good times, it allows you to continue to work harder towards your goals that you have set for yourself. It

THE UPS AND THE DOWNS

is amazing how your creative juices start to flow when things are going well.

Remember, all work and no play leads to a very dull life. So enjoy it, every chance you get.

## Life Is A Journey

Life is a verb, something you are constantly doing. Don't feel like you're stuck when things are down. You aren't. You have the power in you to move things in the direction you need them to move if you stay focused and keep a positive attitude. Don't be afraid to think outside of the box. If you find yourself in a down situation, it is okay to be creative in your choices to get yourself out of that box. You see, life is a journey not a destination.

Now you should be ready to maintain your drive down this road of happiness, whether things are up or down! Now is truly the time to put these ideas into action to start seeing

the results you desire to see: a happy
life.

# 10

# LET'S GET MOVING!

*In the same way, faith by itself, if it is not accompanied by action, is dead.*

—James 2:17

Congratulations, you have made it to the beginning of a new you! You are now armed with some great techniques, tips, and tools to help you achieve the level of happiness that you desire. There are no more excuses. You have no one else to blame. You have the map; you know the direction you should be headed in. The only thing that needs to be done now is for you to start taking the necessary steps outlined in this book. In such a short time you could be living a life beyond even your greatest expectations! I know it is possible. I have done it myself and I have coached others with these same tools.

As you start this journey, I want you to think of this as an action plan to happiness!

## Read It Again

It is not uncommon for us to read something and get great information from it. Yet we tend to forget some of the information that we have learned. It is almost impossible to retain a large amount of information in your head at one time, so revisit this book as often as needed; take notes on what you truly want to work on. This is a great way to help retain the sage advice that you have received.

## Commit To Change

Not too many people like change. It can be scary and difficult for many. You likely have routines that are keeping you unhappy...Know that you are not alone.

However, you must commit to doing whatever is necessary to achieve the level of happiness that you desire. I want you to write this commitment to be happy and to make the changes necessary down like a contract. Have someone else sign it as a witness for you. Tape it to your mirror, frame it, put it on the refrigerator, or any place you know you will look at it each day for a few times a day.

A lot of people read self-help books without making any changes. I don't want you to be one f them. Choose to be happy and fulfilled instead. You will thank yourself later.

## Get A Coach

It always amazes me how professional athletes who are the best in there sports have coaches. These people most of the time are better than their coach. Nevertheless, there is something about having a coach, someone that can hold you accountable and that can help take you to the next level.

Ask a friend or family member to help you monitor your progress. Make sure it is someone that is going to be honest with you and also encouraging. Knowing that you have someone who is cheering you on but also holding you accountable for better or worse will make all the difference in the world.

That is why athletes have coaches. This is why many successful people hire personal, business, and motivational coaches. To be clear, you don't have to go out and hire a coach to achieve this same level of success unless you want to. I will happily avail my own personal coaching services to you, and together we can devise a plan that is certain to take your life to the next level. My contact information will follow this chapter. However, if my services are not a right fit for you or if you simply are not ready for a professional coach, I would encourage you to reach out to someone that you trust. I am positive that your loved ones can do a great job as well.

## Tomorrow Is Not An Option

Don't get this far and think, 'I will get started on this tomorrow'. Tomorrow is not an option. Why start something tomorrow that can be done today? Don't fall for this trap of thinking tomorrow, next week, or next month is the time to start. It is not. Now is the perfect time to start achieving happiness. This book is set up to be immediately applicable so there is zero excuse not to start today!

This is where the real test begins within. It sets the stage for your conscious and subconscious mind to come together to achieve the goals that you have set for yourself.

Do not ignore this time. Real happiness is achievable. Remember, God has great things in store for you!

# Note From The Author

I wanted to take a moment to personally thank you for your purchase of this book. If *Happy?* Has blessed your life and motivated you to be happy, please feel free to visit Amazon.com and leave a review. Thanks, again!

*Sherman Joseph*

# ABOUT THE AUTHOR

Sherman Joseph is sought after around the world for his sage coaching and consultation on how companies, relationships, or someone's spirituality can go to the next level. Sherman has successfully coached and trained CEO's, management staff, entrepreneurs, small business owners, and couples, providing honest, practical, and simple strategies that yield powerful results.

Sherman is passionate about helping his clients find a healthy balance between their professional and personal lives. He believes that true success comes when his clients walk in holistic abundance: physically, mentally, and spiritually.

To learn more about Sherman's books, Blogs, and personal appearances, contact him at:

e-mail: sherman@shermanjoseph.com
website: www.shermanjoseph.com

Also, for daily inspiration to motivate you to Be God's Best You visit:

www.facebook.com/ShermanUJoseph
www.twitter.com/shermanujoseph

# Notes

1. Essence Magazine(2010). Halle berry talks domestic abuse and jenesse center. Retrieved from http://www.essence.com/2010/12/27/halle-berry-talks-domestic-abuse-jenesse-center/
2. Corley, S. (2014, June). *Les brown step into greatness live seminar.* Retrieved from https://www.youtube.com/watch?v=7wBmYlh3ZaM
3. Homann, S.G., Hinton, D.E. & Asnaani, A. (2010). Cultural aspects in social anxiety and social anxiety disorder.US National Library of Medicine Institutes of Health, 27(12), 1117-1127.
4. Oppezzo, M. & Schwartz, D. (2014). Give your ideas some legs: The positive effect of walking on creative thinking. *Journal of Experimental Psychology: Learning, Memory, and Cognition* 40 ( 4), 1142-1152. Retrieved from https://www.apa.org/pubs/journals/releases/xlm-a0036577.pdf

www.ingramcontent.com/pod-product-compliance
Lightning Source LLC
Chambersburg PA
CBHW031342040426
42443CB00006B/441